MOUTHPIECE

PIMPING & PANDERING • HUMAN TRAFFICKING •
CONSPIRACY TO KIDNAP

EAST OAKLAND TIMES, LLC

X
EAST
OAKLAND

"There is no better than adversity. Every defeat, every heartbreak, every loss, contains its own seed, its own lesson on how to improve your performance next time."

El-Hajj Malik El-Shabazz (Malcolm X)

MY CRIME SERIES - BOOK FOUR - MOUTHPIECE

Welcome to Mule Creek State Prison! Come and meet your new "celly." He is a pimp that has a few lessons to teach about growing up on the blood drenched side of Richmond, California, the cut throat psychology of making it in life, and, of course, a breakdown of the pimp's skill set.

Prepare yourself for a raw and uncut verbal onslaught from a young man with a vicious perspective.

The books of the My Crime series are neither meant to justify nor condemn the inmates on whom they are written. Rather, the books of the My Crime series propose to candidly communicate the upbringing, life experience, thoughts, and motivations of the incarcerated.

The My Crime series puts you as the judge. Your judgment will not simply be about the individual on whom a book is written, but your judgment will weigh the life circumstances that shaped his or her criminal disposition. The My Crime series takes the unknown inmate and presents his or her life for public evaluation.

Each book in the My Crime series is written on an inmate, by an inmate. Each book will progress from the Subject's childhood up through the commitment offense that brought about the Subject's current felony incarceration. Each book, therefore, will offer the big picture of the Subject's criminality as dictated to and written by a fellow inmate.

The My Crime series books are intended to fit into the present-day dialog on crime and punishment. As citizens of today's American democracy, the understanding we each have of right and wrong is the essential knowledge we use in taking political positions. Ideally, the justice issued by legislators and interpreted by courts is a justice that agrees with most citizens. If citizens agree with the justice being issued by the government, citizens will promote that justice as truth for the times.

As a society, we do not know ourselves enough to have the right answers on justice.

The My Crime series grants you the opportunity to sit and listen to the unknown felon and learn, as if you were on the bottom bunk, about your neighbor and what brought him or her to getting locked up.

Thank you for purchasing the fourth book in the My Crime series.

Encourage others to read the books in the My Crime series by leaving a review.

I welcome you to visit the webpage dedicated to this series to access additional content for this book and other books in the My Crime series. **Additional content includes phone interviews, book drafts, and supplemental offerings:**

WWW.CRIMEBIOS.COM

Finally, I welcome you to read the last page of this book for information about the producer and publisher of the My Crime series, the East Oakland Times, LLC.

In liberty,

Tio MacDonald
Chief Editor

DISCLAIMER

As this story is being told, I wish to convey that there are some things I am not at liberty to disclose. See, I have an active case and a lot of things I have done in my past are still being investigated. With my case under investigation, I can still be arrested and tried and receive more prison time if pertinent details are revealed in this book. I am not a snitch and I am not here in prison for snitching.

I am not trying to be vague either; it is just that this is the reality of how things are. If you were raised in the streets, then you know where I am coming from. If you are not from the streets then it means that I am not trying to put anyone else in this God forsaken, damn place. Prison will strip you of your heart, soul, and pride if you allow it.

A prison veteran once told me this, "They can cage your body but they can never lock up your mind."

I have chosen to reveal as much as I am both comfortable with and willing to without compromising my morals, principles, and without implicating anyone else.

P.I.M.P

Pimping comes as natural to me as swimming does to a fish, or as soaring comes to an eagle. I am raw and uncut, yet I make absolutely no apologies for it. Abrasiveness is my texture; smoothness is my style. With a sense of me now being felt, I am willing to allow you a larger glimpse into who I am, the world in which I operated, and, in the process, share with you what true pimping is.

In truth, I know that there are a precious few people capable of handling a full view of who I am. Not many of you who read these words will either be willing or objective enough to absorb the realities of the world in which I thrived and flourished.

Pimping means many things to many people. When the majority in society hear the term, they instantly visualize some dude dressed in a cheap ass suit, probably looking like a clown, with a Fedora on. They may think of a guy standing on the street corner with a toothpick sticking out of his mouth and a fur coat on, barking orders to a group of scantily clad, confused, and scared women.

In the real world, pimping is nothing like that.

The acronym P.I.M.P. stands for a variety of things. Here are a few: Power In My Palm, Professional In Manipulating People, Pussy In My Palm, and others. For me P.I.M.P. simply means, Paper In My Pockets.

Money truly does make the world go around. It sets the stage for everything from social class to the perception others have of you. Not that I give a damn about how other people see me or even accept me. Money also opens doors for you that are normally closed. See, there is one truth that is universal; if you don't have money, then you cannot acquire the finer things in life. You cannot sustain yourself. These are lessons I learned at an early age.

2

MENTORS

I was born at Brookside Hospital in San Pablo, California. I lived with my mother. I am her first born child. I have a younger sister and brother with whom I get along with very well. We are all close as a family. Even still, I have not always lived with them.

I define myself as a grandma's boy, meaning I spent a majority of my time with my grandmother. She spoils me to no end, and even now, I know that there is nothing she wouldn't do for me. She has always been my rock. Her love is unconditional and unwavering. No matter where I am, or what I do, I know that my grandma's love is there for me.

Now even though I am a real street person, a product of the rawness in which I lived, I was raised in the church. I had to attend. There was no question about it. Both my mother and grandmother were exceptionally great parents.

Yet, I would not or could not say the same about my sorry ass father. Although I knew where he lived and could have gone to see him or spent time with him whenever I desired, I had no desire whatsoever to do so.

I believe his absence in my life made me a better person. It made me a stronger man. I learned never to depend on anyone for anything. I am self-sufficient. I am a survivor. I am independent. I do not believe in asking for help. If I need it, I go get it. If I cannot get it, and get it for myself, then I do not need it.

Nor do I seek the approval of other people. I could care less what anyone else says or thinks of me. Why should I? I am a grown ass man and not some wide-eyed, wet behind the ears little boy. See a man does what the hell he wants to do and a boy does what he is told to do.

I do not seek out the praises of other people, nor do I spend my time focusing on those who expend their energies hating on me. Again, I ask, why should I?

✖ ✖ ✖

My family lived in Richmond, California until I was three years old; then my mom packed us all up and moved us to Pinole, California. She eventually ended up marrying my sibling's father.

Even at a young age, there was no secret that I didn't want to live with them, so I ended up moving back and forth between their house and Richmond, where I lived with my grandmother. As I mentioned before, my grandma spoiled me and I learned to take full advantage of that. In spite of her spoiling, she had one rule: she said, "If you are going to live in my house, you are going to go to church."

There is no doubt in my mind that my grandma is the one who

taught me how to be a man. She did not sugar coat anything. She worked as a school teacher for twelve years. I used that to my advantage. When I did not want to be in my own class, I would throw a nutty (act out) and my teacher would, to calm me, send me to my grandma's class. I still was not allowed to just sit around. I would do the work her classroom was assigned. My grandma taught me to work for what I wanted and to be a go-getter.

She eventually switched careers and became a lunch lady. I saw that no matter what, she was a hustler in the sense that she took care of her business. She eventually retired.

Now let me state, I had a relatively smooth upbringing, even before my mother gave birth to my siblings yet we still started struggling and ended up on welfare, receiving food stamps and living in section eight housing. Eventually, things grew bad between my mother and her husband and he ended up leaving her with three kids to care for on her own.

As I think on this, I can say that both my mother and grand-mother were prime examples for me of what a loyal woman, a true woman, a dedicated woman, is. They are sparkling exam-ples of the definition of a woman with values and morals. They taught me that for a woman to value a man, that woman must value herself first and foremost.

If a woman does not respect herself, if she disregards her own appearance and wellbeing, then you cannot expect for her to do those things to or for you. So, there is no doubt that my grandma and my mother's teachings, even when they had no idea that they were doing so, were the catalyst for my views on life.

Likewise, seeing my mom's struggles shaped my personality. Her struggles solidified my views of the world. It is about taking care of myself and my family by any means necessary. See, it is clear cut, you are either with me or against me. And, if you are not with me, then I am going to make it my business to roll right over you. So, if you are on the opposite side of me then it is in your best interest to get the hell out of my way.

I also believe that if you are down for me, then I will be down for you. I help those who help me. If you push me, then I will pull you and vice versa. If you are loyal to me, then I am, without a doubt, loyal to you. When you are living a street life, that is just how it has to be. If not, then others are going to walk all over you.

✖ ✖ ✖

When it comes to my dad, well, I really do not have much to say about that nigger except fuck him! I feel this way because he knew who I was and where I was, but he never lifted a finger to help me. Nor did he make any type of effort to be in my life. As a man, and as a father, he should have fought harder for me, the way I do to remain in my own children's lives. Honestly, what does it say about him as a man if he will not even fight for his own flesh and blood?

Yet in spite of this, I can say that I did learn a couple of things from his sorry ass. For one, I learned how to be man enough not to run from my responsibilities, like he did. After all, running away does not stop the responsibilities from being there. Also, I learned in part, how to get my hustle on. I learned to drive hard to get what I want. See, the one thing my father did was, he didn't let anything stand in his way or stop him, not even his kids. He is the true definition of a go-getter. In a way, he taught me just like my grandma did, but in a different way.

✖ ✖ ✖

I moved to Texas when I was about nine years old and I stayed for a year. I went there with my mom and her boyfriend. It was too much for me in the sense that even at that young of an age, I missed the streets of Richmond, so I returned. Texas just wasn't for me. I knew I needed to be in the middle of the action. I needed to be where things were happening.

✖ ✖ ✖

The main influence in my life was my uncle. Although my drive and hustle came from my dad and grandma, my uncle was the main force in shaping my attitude. He was in the streets and did everything the streets offered. He was, by far, the truest definition of a hustler. By that, I mean that any and everything that crossed his hands, he sold. Drugs, CD's, DVD's, anything, he pushed. Hell, he was even a stripper. His stripping names were "Mello Mel" and "Taste of Chocolate."

He was also a pimp in the truest sense of the word. Yes, he sent hoes to go and get his paper, but he also carried guns and was a force to be reckoned with. I watched on many occasions as he both talked his way into and out of shit all the time. I have even seen him driving a cab at one point just to get his paper.

Once, he rode me around in his car and gave me a gun. He pointed to someone walking down the streets and said, "Okay, you want to be with this street life shit? Well go out there and get with it and come back with everything in that nigger's pockets." Needless to say, I did just that and it was an exciting feeling and an experience I will never forget.

✖ ✖ ✖

I realized at an early age that I wasn't good at stealing, unlike many of my friends. I remember once when my grandma, my mother, and I, went to a store. While they were preoccupied, I stole a black and brown toy cap gun. I managed to walk out of the store and got away with it. Excited about my accomplishment, I showed it to my mother, who was none too pleased. She, in turn, showed it to my grandmother. My grandmother took me back to the store and made me give the gun back.

Somehow, I found myself in front of a police officer. He sat me down and talked to me. I don't remember everything he said, but I do remember him asking me what I had learned from the situation: "I learned that I do not like my grandma or the police," I said.

I also remember my mother telling me that she would not have told on me but that the gun looked too real. I never thought that that was a good enough reason.

3

STREET ETHICS

There is no one defining moment, one crystal clear point of reference that I can pinpoint and say, "Ah-ha, that is the time when I first learned about crime." Crime has always been an intricate part of my life. It has always had a prevalent presence in the environment in which I grew up.

It was nothing out of the ordinary for me to see someone selling drugs, smoking weed, getting high, or being robbed on a regular basis. Many of the people doing the selling, smoking, and robbing were people I knew and hung out with.

Stealing was as commonplace as breathing. No one really gave much ethical thought to the fact that we were stealing. It was just something that we did. Most of the time, it was to survive. Some people stole to have food to eat. Some did it to have nice clothes to wear and sometimes people stole just because whatever it was that they were stealing, was there.

The fact that my mother was not able to give me the things I wanted was definitely a contributing factor in my criminal ventures. Wanting to keep pace with all of the things my friends seemed to have, gave me the motivation I needed to go out and get it at any cost. I was definitely trying to keep up with the "Joneses." I knew that the streets held what I needed and I knew that the only way I could lay my hands on it was by getting in the streets and taking it.

✖ ✖ ✖

Like stealing and other crimes, violence, in almost every sense of the word, has been a significant part of my life. Everything from fighting to seeing someone get popped (shot) and lose his life, has been common. I have seen dudes beat their women and I have seen dudes getting beat down by other dudes. I have seen groups of girls take off on a single girl just because they hated that she looked better or that she was more popular. Hell, I have had to handle my own business on many occasions. I have had to bust (shoot) on some dudes as well.

I was probably around ten years old when I got into a fight with someone because I was protecting my cousin. See, this Mexican guy was bagging (making jokes) on my cousin and my cousin couldn't take it. My mom, she's a real thug, told me, "Go outside and beat his ass baby." I knew I had to do it or suffer the consequences and get my own ass whipped. I knew my mom wasn't making idle threats. So, I did exactly that, I went outside and beat the hell out of the dude.

ANGER MANAGEMENT

One thing that is an asset for me is that I have never been the type of person to let my temper rule me. I rule over it. I can be furious with someone, even to the point of wanting to kill that person, but he would never know because I will keep my anger under wraps.

I will admit that there has been a time or two when I did succumb and let anger get the best of me. Most times I will think rationally and play things out in my head. I will examine the wide variety of options to a situation and decide which would be the best course of action. Then, there are times that I won't. I will just let myself go. I will simply react. I will allow myself to give in to the rage that floods me and let my anger run its course.

Being from where I am from, Richmond, California, you have to be like this. It is a way of life. Sometimes words are not enough. Sometimes, words just don't get through to people. Sometimes, they only understand one language: they only understand the language of violence.

There were times when I would be all gung-ho. I would be like, fuck it, and say let's just go all out. I would feel like there was no need for talking. I would only desire to get things started. To be engrossed in violence.

For the most part, and as an adult, I realize that I now have far too much to lose. Plus, I know that time thinking is time well spent. Yes, there are times when you have to just do what you have to do to survive, and times when you have to just not give a damn to survive. You have to live life. The best bet is to plan things out and execute them in a way so you assure yourself the best of outcomes.

UNREQUITED LOVE

The first time I can say that I ever truly had my heart broken was also the last time that I allowed myself to be gullible and be in that situation. It was the last time I got my heart broken.

I was around thirteen and was infatuated with this girl, I mean I really liked her. I was all in. Unfortunately, many young men are vulnerable at that age, and some even carry this type of mindset into their adult years.

Still, it was clear that she never felt the same way towards me. While I was busy being all caught up and blinded by love, and while I was playing the square role, the hoe was out getting money for some other dude. I was being a real simp. Not only that, I actually walked in and caught her having sex with one of my partners. That alone showed me how scandalous females truly are. They are the sneakiest species on the face of this earth. Thus, I have adopted the motto, "Never trust a bitch!"

Now I keep my heart shut down. I keep it locked away and refuse to allow it exposure to such weak, false feelings. See, before I ever put my all into a woman again, she is going to have to go all out to prove herself worthy of me. She is going to have to show me that she is someone who can contribute to me. She has to show me what she can bring to the table. She is going to have to go above and beyond the call of duty.

Common-sense dictates that all women are not hoes, and I know this. But, I also know that all women have hoe tendencies. I do not think that such tendencies are a bad thing. Most women are just too shy to act on those feelings. It just takes the right man at the right time to bring it out of them. All they need is the right guidance. They need a hand to lead the way.

6

A TURNING POINT

I really started acting out violently when I was fourteen. It was a conscious decision on my part.

Two of my partners and I broke into a house and stole three guns. We each took one. After that, I started thinking I was John Gotti. I felt that way because, before I had my own gun, I used to hold guns for my uncle. Age fourteen marked the first time I shot at someone. It was one of the most euphoric experiences I have ever had. It was a rush like none other.

We were out walking and doing what we did, just hanging out and talking shit to each other, smoking weed and bragging about all the hoes we were having sex with. This was about three days after we had stolen the guns. We noticed a car circling the block. It did this several times. One of my homies said, "If that damn car hits the block one more time, we need to light it up." Sure enough, the car came around the corner once more. Just as it passed by us, all three of us pulled out our guns and let loose. We lit the car up.

✖ ✖ ✖

It wasn't long before I started feeling like the entire world was against me. Everyone started showing their true colors. They were all about them, so I consciously made the shift in my mind to start being all about me. I always put me first. That was one of the best decisions I could have ever made in my life.

MOUTHPIECE MAGIC

My teenage years were when my frame of thinking really started to take shape. I was already becoming independent in that I was not living with my mom or anyone. I stayed out and hung out with my homies and basically did me. Meaning, I did whatever in the hell I wanted to with no questions asked.

Thinking back, I was around fourteen when I realized for the first time, that words can either make or break someone. I came to understand that the things I said held a power unlike anything else. With this knowledge, it was not long before I began to see that saying the right thing, to the right person, could get me whatever I wanted in life.

I once watched my uncle talk a female out of her whole check. I thought to myself, "Man, this is amazing." I loved it. I love the way a female can be believing the stuff you are saying. I knew that every word my uncle said to the lady was a lie, but she was hanging on to his every word, as if for dear life. She was going through all sorts of emotional changes. She was completely caught up. It was then that I realized something profound. See, if you can lie good enough to the point that you believe your own lie, then it is easy as hell to get someone else to believe it.

The amazing thing is, this isn't some new concept or an out of the ordinary perception. In fact, it happens every day in every conception of life, all over the world. It happens especially in this country in courthouses during trials.

The prosecutors and defense attorneys do this for a living. They both tell their version of a story, most of what is said by both sides are lies. The one who lies the most convincingly, the one that is most believable, wins over the jury.

Now granted, sometimes the story, the different versions of it, will be sprinkled with a few facts, just to lend credence to the telling, but for the most part, it is all speculation.

✖ ✖ ✖

I was going on fifteen when I officially started living on my own. Up until then, I was basically going back and forth from my mom's to my grandma's, and on occasion, spending a couple of days with one girl or another.

When I started doing shit for myself, I experienced a whole new level of independence. I felt liberated. My mom wanted me home and I wanted to be in the streets. I decided to do things my way and ended up in the streets full time. I was going all out.

I am a self-assured person. I only depend on one person and that is myself. If I make a wrong decision then that is on me. I make no excuses. I view each lesson as God's blessing. I take my own chances and make my own choices.

It is like, a person will jump into the ocean and start swimming, knowing that the water is filled with sharks. Even so, he will still do it. He takes a chance, and in some way, gets an absolute thrill out of it, out of making that choice. That is how I am. I take my own chances.

SCHOOL AIN'T SHIT

The last grade I attended in school was either the tenth or eleventh. I am not quite sure. I was, however, what one would consider an overachiever.

In my classes, whenever I chose to go, I had all A's and B's. I knew the work but hated doing any form of homework. I enjoyed clowning around, having fun with my friends and, of course, smoking weed. I loved the attention girls gave me. The fact that I knew I could get anything I wanted out of them by just saying the right things, made the challenge of getting something from them even more satisfying.

A lot of the time, I would just sit around with my partners and just shoot dice and talk shit about people. It was during some of these "clowning" sessions when the truth would really hit you because the things we said were raw and uncut. We would show our asses. If you were dressed like a bum, we would talk shit about you. If your hair was nappy or your breath stank, we would clown you about it. School was nothing more than a fashion show for most of us.

Feelings were never a factor. If you were working with feelings and wanted to get all butt hurt, and if you felt as if you wanted to do something about it, then you would just get your ass kicked.

KEEN ON DRUGS

The first time I used any type of drugs, I was around eleven or twelve years old. I had a friend who was bi-racial, half Mexican and half white. He was hella cool, but the crazy thing is, his grandmother was a stone-cold racist.

It was over at his house that I met his sister, who I was trying to have sex with, and she gave me my first taste of weed. She rolled up a blunt and shared it with me. I felt relaxed. I remember thinking that it was the best feeling in the world. I vowed that if I could get past my mother, I would be smoking weed each and every single day. Even now, I love myself some good weed.

I was fourteen when I guess you can say I graduated from weed. I started sipping syrup. Syrup is simply Promethazine and Codeine, or cough syrup. I also started doing prescription pills, mainly Narcos, Vicodins, Percocets, and on a few occasions, a mixture of them together. They are all opioids. I also started doing ecstasy. I had seen other people popping them and finally thought, "Why the hell not?" Ecstasy was an awesome experience. I never graduated from doing it. I just got locked up and can't get my hands on any.

✖ ✖ ✖

W hen it comes to drugs, there are two categories: drugs to be up, hyper, and moving at a million miles a minute and drugs to be down. These drugs are known as downers. They are relaxed, chill, and basically mellowed out. I prefer downers. Ecstasy is an upper. When I am down, I don't get into trouble. I stay mellow. I am cool and kicked back. I am relaxed. It is the same with heroin. The amount you take effects just how mellow you are.

The thing about heroin is, I never actually tried it when I was out on the streets. It was only when I came to prison that I began to indulge. One of the reasons I like downers is because when I am in such a relaxed state, it reminds me of when I was out on the streets. It is an escape for me, and it takes me away from prison.

There are not too many words I can use to describe prison except that is unlike anything on earth. There is nothing but a bunch of tough ass acting dudes, strutting around, acting like they can't be touched by anything or anyone. There is far too much testosterone and not enough relief.

Although many people find their relief in either cards, fighting, or other means, I, on the other hand, find my relief in getting high. I get faded, workout, and talk a gang of shit. I kick it with a few select people, and then, I only do that on occasion.

CAREER PROSPECTS

I was never good at selling dope, although I tried doing it for a few rounds. I remember I got into it with this one female. I was probably around fourteen or fifteen. She gave me five G's (grams) of cocaine but, as I said, I wasn't too good at selling it, so I just did whatever was needed to get it off me. I was selling the stuff dirt cheap. To be totally honest, I was more focused on getting money from her.

FIRST TIME GETTING SHOT

No matter what I chose to do, violence has always been around me. I have been stabbed a few times, by my babies' mothers, and I have been shot twice.

The first time I was shot I was either fifteen or sixteen years old. I was fortunate that the bullet only grazed me on my left hip. At the time, I was half-ass pimping. Thinking that I was the man, basically feeling myself. I also thought I was invincible. There were about six or seven of us just hanging out in front of my great-grandmother's house smoking weed, drinking, and talking shit to each other like we always did. She lived on the south side of Richmond. All of a sudden, a car came around the corner and someone inside started letting off (firing shots at the group of us). We scattered and started running in every direction. I don't know exactly when it happened because I was jumping fences and bending corners as fast as I could. It wasn't until I actually looked down and saw the blood covering the left side of my shirt that it dawned on me that I was shot. That was when it began to hurt.

When I got to my mom's house, I didn't mention being shot. I just put some alcohol on the wound and bandaged it up until the bleeding stopped. I knew that if my mom found out, she would have whipped my ass. Plus, I had no desire to hear her ranting and raving, knowing that it would go on for days.

The amazing thing is, being shot seemed to make me even more popular with women. They catered to me and of course, I ate all the attention up and used it to my advantage.

UNCLE KILLED

I was fifteen when one of the hardest and most hurtful things I have ever had to face happened: my uncle was killed in front of me. He was shot by the San Pablo police. He didn't have a gun or any other kind of weapon on him. That was the moment I knew in my heart that I hated the police. They took from me the one person who was like a father.

His death helped turn my heart cold and made me embrace a "fuck the world" attitude. That is the attitude I hold to this day.

13

ROMANCE

I recall going to school and this one girl was really trying to come at me with some negative type of hype saying she was better than me because I was wearing the same outfit that I had worn the day before. Instead of feeling bad about it, I pulled out a wad of cash and flashed it at her. She was stuck. She couldn't do anything but respect that. From then on, the females were all on me.

I was seventeen when I met one of the first women I can say I was captivated by. Her name was Lea. She was living in a section of Richmond, California known as the "Kennedy Manor." She was light skinned with green eyes and had the most perfect set of lips a woman could hope to ever have. I mean this woman really had me stuck.

I loved everything about her. I loved her vibe. She was down to earth, loyal, understanding, and had this quiet confidence. Yet, she allowed me to be me. She wasn't trying to change me in any way.

I still recall the clothes she had on the first time I met her. That is how powerful of an effect she had on me. She was wearing these sexy little shorts. In my mind and heart, I knew that I had to have her. In fact, I wasn't the only one caught up in her aura. Everybody was trying to get at her. All of them were trying to have sex with her, but she was not having it.

Yet, when they all gave up, I pressed on. That was the day that I learned a very valuable lesson. I learned that persistence is the key to life. Whatever you want or want to do, you have to keep at it. You got to keep going. Failure cannot be an option.

Lea eventually left Richmond and went back to Oregon, but came back one month later. When she did, my persistence paid off and she became mine.

✖ ✖ ✖

The thing is, I never really did the girlfriend thing, especially not the high school girls. I tried to talk to them but quickly realized that they just weren't on my level. I even tried to get them to drop out of school and start ho'ing for me, but they wouldn't. Ironically, most of them are now actually ho'ing, but they don't do it for me.

LACE YOU UP ON THIS PIMP GAME

One absolute truth is that pimping is a major business. It is like Home Depot, or IBM, or McDonald's. See, Ronald McDonald is not actually at any of the thousands of Mickey D's around the world. He is not the one working all those long, grueling hours. He is not the one doing those tiring double shifts. Nor has he ever done all the back-breaking labor that is required. No, Ronald is never there.

Like any major business or corporation, the grunts, the minions, the slave laborers, are the ones who are on the grind. They are the ones who shoulder the burdens and do all the work. They are the ones who are responsible for bringing in the money. Just like Ronald, it is my duty to get paid off of a hoe's labor.

Now the first time I realized that this pimping game was really for me, I was around sixteen years old. One of my "OG" (original gangster) homies got at me about how I was doing things. He said, "Youngster, you are out here selling dope and taking all these chances, and for what? You are doing all this for some chump change."

He went on. "You got bitches coming up to you, bringing you food and anything else you want. Why not have them getting you your money too?" He went on to lace me about the pimping game.

He said, "It is like this, you got at least fifty who are feeling you. Now let's just say you approach them all about ho'ing for you. Half of them off the top are not going to be with it, or even want to hear what you have to say about it. So, that leaves you with twenty-five who seem as if they are willing to hear you out.

"Out of that twenty-five, fifteen will really take in what you are saying and really hear you, or even vibe with you. Seven or eight of them will actually listen to what you say and take it to heart.

"Now out of these seven or eight, at least three will actually go out and try to get that paper for you. Now of those three, you have to use your mind and pick one to go on the road with you. You make her your down ass bottom bitch. You take off from there and do your thing."

Now I want to say this, a pimp is what the world wants to label him as. I label myself as an entrepreneur. I believe in getting my money by any means necessary. God blessed me with a mouth-piece and the ability to get people to see my point of view. I am able to get people to see me and understand what I am saying.

I have been blessed to be surrounded by women who want to see me come up, women who want to see me flourish. I have been fortunate to have women who want to see me winning. And, not only that, they want to be there with me as I am winning.

See, the reality is, a lot of people in this world talk about love, but when the bills are due, or when there is no food on the table, or no money in your pockets, I'd like to see you pay them bills with love. I would like to see you getting your empty stomach full with a plate of love. I would like to see you fill your pockets with love and spend that instead of money.

Love is just a word that suckas use to justify being weak. Love is something people claim in order to feel good about being all sensitive.

Now you got a lot of these loose ass women out in the world just having sex with numerous dudes for free. They are doing it for nothing. The only thing they are getting is a nutt. Many of these women are contracting STD's and they are carefree about it. They spend more time in the clinic than they do in school, or in church, or even at their jobs if they have one. They are taking more pills and shots trying to get rid of the stuff they are catching than a pharmacy can supply.

If you are laying up with just one man I can commend you for that. If you are holding him down and doing the monogamous thing, then that's cool. Hell, even if you are the type of woman who has two men, and you are doing your thing with them, I can even respect that. After all, sometimes a person needs one or two lovers to help sate the appetite.

Then, you have all these women who just go around having sex with multiple men. They are so loose that they can't even keep up with all the men they are laying down with.

The truth is, if you are going to be doing all this screwing with all these men, hell, you might as well get paid for it. After all, why not? Hoes are running around here with major back pain because they are always laying on their backs with their legs cocked open. They are talking in high pitched voices because they are having so much oral sex it is probably shoving their tonsils in their throat.

So, if you are going to be doing all of this extra duty, you may as well start getting paid for it. You might as well benefit from all your hard labor.

✖ ✖ ✖

I have earned my money by being a go-getter. Yes, people label me as a pimp because I get my money out of a hoe's ass, but the truth is, I can't stop a woman from believing in me and my dreams, and wanting to help me get there.

See, a lot of people believe in a lot of things. Some people believe in religion. Some people believe in science. Some people believe in myths. But, I learned at a very young age to get people to believe in me.

I don't see myself in any special way or order. I see myself as a determined person who strives for success. I work hard to win. I push the envelope to the limits with the only goal being, to come out on top.

See, the white man has been winning since the dawn of time. He has most of the power and he wields it to his advantage. Well, I want to win off of him, just like he has been winning off of me and my people all these years. Plus, pimping is a hustle and it is my favorite thing to do. It is fun, exciting, challenging, and cool.

So, then why not hustle and get my money from some good-looking women? Especially, when they are willing to help me get it. Why not come up?

✖ ✖ ✖

I hated selling drugs and the one main reason for that is I hate for weird ass people to come up to me. I am somewhat anti-social, yet at the same time, if I am put into a room filled with women, I will shine as bright as the noonday sun. I will bling like brand new money.

Plus, there is no one method to pimping. It is not as if there is a singular blueprint or course that you have to follow. Plus, I have always been good at talking myself into and out of various situations. With that being a truth, then what is so wrong with me talking myself into some money? If a woman is willing to handle her business for me, then I am going to get my money.

I am sure that everyone has heard the old saying, "A closed mouth don't get fed." The Bible says, "Ask and ye shall receive." So that is what I do. I ask women to go out and handle business for me; they do, and come back with that money and I gratefully receive it.

✖ ✖ ✖

I would not be able to keep an accurate account of all the times someone has come up to me and asked me if pimping is about sex. The answer to that is hell no!

And for the record, it is not about beating down a woman either. Pimping is strictly BUSINESS! It is about getting paid. It is about enjoying the fruits of your labor. It is about being a successful business person.

I use the term fruits of your labor because it is hard work honing the pimp craft. There are a lot of haters in this world. Most of them are gunning for you and trying to keep you down. They hate to see me winning. But, they can't stop me because winning is what I do best. It is in my make-up. It flows through my veins. It is in my blood. I am a winner because I am a real nigga.

Women are beautiful. They have a magnetism about themselves, but very few are really capable of tapping into their inner essence. That is what I do. I connect with their inner-energy and help bring it to the surface. I am like their guide.

FIRST CHILD

I was seventeen when I met my first baby's mother. She is the mother of my son. I met her after I had already met Lea. I met her at a mutual friend's home. In fact, it was my cousin who introduced the two of us to each other.

At the time, I had a different style than I have now. I wore my hair in locks and I even went by a different name. I went by the name Hyphie, which was given to me by my cousin, the cousin that introduced me to my son's mom. He was known as Hyphie as well.

But, I also had the name because it fit me. I was a hyper person. I was all over the place and I was honing my "I-don't-give-a-fuck" attitude. I didn't give a damn about anything or anyone.

I remember how she walked into the house and smiled. She had a charm about her. We chilled and ended up smoking some weed. We connected on a deeper level and our love for each other grew.

A ROBBERY GONE WRONG

Now even though I was connecting with my baby's mother (BM), I was still out there doing my own thing. I was still committed to thugging.

When I turned eighteen, I went to jail for robbery. I was with three of my partners. I was the oldest and the youngest was sixteen. I had gotten an inside scoop from this chick I knew on a lick (job.) A dude was papered up (carrying a lot of cash on him) and we planned to rob him. I found out the time and place where he was going to be and I got with my boys and set things in motion.

We walked from my aunt's house to the BART (Bay Area Rapid Transit) station, then made our way to the target's house. I noticed that the guy's car was not parked at his house. I decided that the mission was going to be bust and we headed back towards the BART station.

Now out of the whole crew, I was the only one with a weapon. I had a high point .40 caliber handgun. I had no problem with using it if it came down to it.

On the way to the BART station, we saw an older lady walking. One of my partners asked if we should rob her. I didn't think she had any money on her so I wasn't too interested in wasting time on her. In spite of this, my boys went off to rob her. I walked to the corner of the street and turned around to tell them to quit wasting their time and to catch up to me. I noticed that they had already started trying to rob the lady and she was fighting back. In fact, she was actually winning the battle. She was giving them a run for their money so to speak. Eventually, they ran off and ran past me. I took off with them.

I was so angry I could hardly think straight. In fact, I was so mad I actually thought about just shooting them right then and there. Hell, not only did they get their asses whipped by an old lady, she only had one dollar and a credit card on her. My anger boiled over and eventually, we all started to argue.

I had my phone on me and we stopped arguing when it rang. It was one of my old hoes calling to tell me she was about to have a baby and she needed money fast. I snatched the dollar and the credit card from my boy's hand and something told me to look back at where the old lady was. I noticed that she was talking on a phone as well. I immediately took off running again.

The entire time that I was running I was talking on the phone. I raced through the BART station, not really knowing where I was going. The police arrived and ended up chasing me. I was doing everything in my power to shake them, but nothing was working. I was jumping over fences like I was an Olympic high jumper. In fact, I ripped my left hand so badly that it required six stitches. Amazingly, the entire time, I was not even worried about the ripped hand or the blood that was pouring out of the wound. I was too focused on running and worried about my pregnant hoe.

I ran for about an hour, but in the end, it didn't do any good. The police had cornered off the entire block and there was no getting around it. Knowing that there wasn't much of a chance of me getting away, I tossed my gun under a parked car.

After all the running around and so much blood loss, my legs gave out on me. Even still, I wasn't just going to give up. I struggled with a female cop. She suddenly fired my shit up (hit me hard). I hit the ground and ended up scaring up my face.

I was charged with robbery. The victim pointed me out and lied on me saying that I was the one who had actually robbed her. I ended up staying in jail for eight days before I managed to bail out. At court, they labeled me a menace to society. I ended up doing a month on house arrest and was forced to wear an ankle monitor.

17

SECOND CHILD

I was twenty-one when I met my second baby's mother. She is the mother of my first daughter. I met her through my cousin James. He's from a part of Vallejo, California known as "The Crest." It was made famous by the rapper Mac Dre.

James called me one day saying that he wanted us to play basketball. At the time, I had a Lexus Coupe SC 400 and a Dodge Charger. Now although a lot of my homies did this, I never was the type of person to go joy riding in stolen cars. I knew that joy riding was one of the quickest ways to wind up locked behind bars. On this kind of street knowledge, I was laced tight by my uncle. He was like a sensei with all the under-standing of the streets he had. For example, I was never one to actually rob anyone. I always let the people I was with actually do the robbing. I would just end up getting half of whatever was taken. I always talked other gullible people into doing the actual crime. I had the gift of gab and knew how to use it to my advantage.

Anyway, I went to pick up my cousin James. When he jumped into the car, I asked him at whose house he was kicking it. He told me that it was his aunt's and that she actually wanted to meet me. He said that she had heard a lot of things about me and needed to see if the things she had heard about me were true.

When I walked into the house, I noticed this skinny, young, sexy woman watching James and me. She and I eventually started talking and that, of course, led to us smoking weed. After some time had passed, I asked James where was his aunt who wanted to meet me. I was shocked when he pointed to the same woman I had been talking and smoking with the entire time.

I knew then and there that I had to have her. I had never had a woman who was so interested in my conversation. I was breathing on her like a brand-new fan. (Breathing means I was really putting my game down. I was handling my business.)

I eventually got around to asking her who she was living with and was pleasantly surprised when she told me that she owned her own home. Needless to say, my interest piqued higher than it had been before. The more we talked, the more I learned. She eventually revealed that there was a guy in her past that she was trying to get away from. I was going to make it my business to see to it that she did.

She was the only woman in my life to ever make me wait three or four months before we had sex. Yet instead of that being a bother to me, it not only made things more interesting; it also gave me a deeper respect for her. I knew that she wasn't like any other woman and I was determined to have her in my life at all times, by any means necessary. So, to assure myself of this, I put a baby in her. Even up to this day, she holds a piece of my heart.

18

SHOT AGAIN

I was around twenty-two when I got shot for the second time. I was out spending time with this female who was basically giving me money. I had worked some things out to where every month, the bank was giving me almost three bands (three thousand dollars.) It wasn't much, just a little chump change I used to buy guns and some syrup to sip.

I asked my mom to take me to a bank branch in Alameda, about twenty miles from Richmond. Now I could have gone to any branch of this particular bank and collected my money, but I am meticulous and only wanted to use the bank branch in Alameda.

Reluctantly, my mom agreed. However, the entire time we were in the car, she was ranting and raving about how I was out in the streets too much and needed to slow down. She was preaching about how I needed to stop doing the stuff I was doing and get my life together.

Needless to say, I had no desire to hear all of her complaining. It got so bad that I just asked her to drop me off at my cousin's house, which of course, she refused to do. In fact, she demanded that I listen to her.

Eventually, it became so overwhelming that I threatened to just jump out of the car at the next light if she did not stop her talk. Finally, she relented and took me to my cousin's. Before she left, I gave her a few dollars which she gladly took from me.

✖ ✖ ✖

At my cousin's, I immediately started smoking weed as soon as I entered the house. They were already blazing and getting high, yet that was nothing out of the ordinary. Eventually, I got around to asking my cousin to take me to the bank. He was reluctant but relented. His one demand was that I leave my gun at the house. Now leaving my gun was something that I just didn't do, and I normally would have had a fit just because he asked, but I gave in because he said that he would take his gun instead.

We did argue over who would do the driving. He had a two-door Benz and I was dying to get behind the wheel. Of course, with it being his car, he won that argument. So, to relax, I stretched out in the back seat with my head laying on the window. I am not sure how long I laid there because I was high. Now one truth about driving is that whoever is doing the driving is supposed to watch the rearview mirror. The driver is the eyes of the car. He is supposed to be paying the most attention. Obviously, my cousin was not doing that. Suddenly, out of nowhere, something told me to look back. When I did, all I saw was this dude driving his car right beside us pointing a gun directly at me with an "I got yo' ass" smile on his face. Just as I was about to yell out a warning, the guy pulled the trigger and I got hit in the mouth. The bullet went through my lip, then through my teeth and then through my tongue and came out on the opposite side. I was fortunate that I had a mouth full of gold and diamonds.

The guy lit the car up. He shot at us thirty-three times including the one that hit me in the mouth. I later found out that I had been shot with a nine-millimeter. My cousin immediately started shooting back. We got off the freeway and my cousin drove me to the hospital. I didn't have any form of bandages except for my coat so I held that to my face, in an attempt to stop the bleeding. The pain was intense.

Once in the emergency room, I had difficulty telling them what had happened to me, and that I had been shot. Blood was by now, everywhere. The security guard, who was inside the emergency room, finally understood what I was trying to say and ran to locate a doctor. I was placed on a gurney but refused to lay down, in spite of all of their efforts to get me to do so. They had no idea that each time I did, I was choking. The nurse was insistent so I reached into my mouth and took out the bullet and threw it at her.

During the course of all the commotion, I called my baby's mother, who eventually ended up understanding me enough and she called my mother. I was taken and prepped for surgery. The only thing I remember after that was a nurse standing over me and instructing me to count backward from one hundred. I made it to ninety-nine and was out cold.

I woke in a room at John Muir's Hospital. I saw that my mom was in the room. She eventually turned on the news and I found out that there were four shootings in Richmond that night. That was when I realized that the homies loved me for real. All of the shootings were done in retaliation for what had happened to me.

It took about three months before the swelling went down enough for me to be able to open my mouth. I was fortunate in that the bullet did not shatter my jaw, but it did fracture it. Even to this day, it has not completely healed.

19

THIRD CHILD

I met my third baby's mother when I was twenty-three. She is the definition of a computer love. I say this because I met her on Instagram. She was so sexy to me. I had no problem letting her black ass know exactly how I felt.

I was bold and direct with her and asked her if I could have her. I even recall what I said. I said, "I like chocolate. Can I have a piece of you?"

She is extremely dark. She laughed and told me how funny she thought I was. We spent time chatting and eventually I asked for her number. We talked for like three or four days.

Now at the time, I didn't have a car. I wanted to go and buy some weed, so I called her and asked if she had a car. She told me that she did. I then made her a proposition: I told her that if she took me to Sacramento to buy some weed, I not only would smoke with her, but I would feed her and whomever else she brought with her. I also agreed to put gas in her car; I ended up filling the car up.

All the time we were on our way to Sac. we talked and started getting to know each other even better. Well, we ended up smoking some good ass weed and getting high and I eventually asked her to spend the night with me. Of course, we began to have sex. It was during the course of this that I stopped and asked her if she wanted to be with me for the rest of her life. She said yes, so I took off the condom I had on and we continued to have sex. Afterward, I told her that she now belonged to me for the rest of her life.

She had my second daughter while I was incarcerated fighting this case. She held me down all the way until she "frogged the fuck off." For those of you who do not know what that means, it means when someone claims to be loyal, real, and all that bullshit, then leaves you when you need her the most.

✖ ✖ ✖

It is crazy because deep down inside, a part of me always knew that hoes ain't shit. That is why my motto is dog them out before they get the chance to dog you.

See, the hoe got close to me and warmed up my icebox (my heart.) She thawed me out, then threw me back out. Now I got frostbite. But, I am not tripping, because I know that hoes are not loyal nor are they truly about shit.

The crazy thing is, even though I am talking a lot of shit about all of my children's mothers, they are all good to my kids. They take care of their motherly responsibilities. They put my kids before anything else and that is how it should be. Plus, on top of that, they are committed to bringing my kids up here to this God forsaken place to see me whenever they are not on some dumb line of thinking.

As I look back, I can say that some of the happiest moments of my life were having my kids. I was eighteen when I had my first child. He was born in 2008. My second was born when I was twenty-two, in 2012. My third was born when I turned twenty-four in 2014, but, as I mentioned, I was incarcerated.

20

MY CRIME

I am currently in prison for human trafficking, which is some real bullshit. My definition of human trafficking is when you are manhandling a hoe. Human trafficking is when you are throwing a bitch in the trunk of a car or something, with her hands and feet tied up and a gag in her mouth, driving her all over the world and forcing her to have sex with any and everybody who is willing to pay.

Now if a hoe is well aware of what is going on and chooses to participate, if she jumps in the car willingly, then that is not human trafficking. The real issue is when Uncle Sam is not getting a piece of the action; when the government is not getting a cut, then it is considered a crime. But, when Uncle Sam can place his greasy ass palms on the money, then it is all good. Hell, just look at Nevada. It is known as the "hoe state." It is all good and legal to go and get a prostitute, but that is because the government is getting a nice piece of the action.

And, on top of that, everyone knows that the criminal justice system is rigged. That is no big secret. And, it is rigged to keep the minority population down, especially the black man. Race is not just about color. It is also about social status.

Now even with that being said, I do not think that racism was a major factor in my case, but politics definitely was. If you do not have a paid lawyer, then you are just assed out. I know I got played. I was used as a stepping stone.

Now as I mentioned earlier, my case is still active and in the courts, so there are not too many things that I can go into detail about. But I can say, I am in here for pimping and pandering, conspiracy to kidnap, and as I mentioned, human trafficking.

Now what I can say is that they have me in here on some real bullshit. They have me locked up for pimping a hoe I do not even know. A bitch I never even sent to the grocery store, so I damn sure I never sent her out to go turn a trick. She is a person I met for the first time in my life, and as a result, I am now locked up for the rest of my life!

✖ ✖ ✖

The worst moments for me are each and every moment I am caged like an animal in this place and taken away from society. I am being taken from my duties as a father. It does not take a lifetime to rehabilitate a person. Anyone of reasonable, common sense, can rehabilitate within a five-year span. By keeping a person caged up for life, the system is trying to strip you of your soul. Prison is a money-making business. It is pimping at its finest.

The reality is, nothing is going to change. You have people out in society fighting tooth and nail to free a caged animal, yet would probably never lift a finger to help free a human being.

21

MY LEGACY

Two of my fondest memories are when I cut the umbilical cords on my first two kids. I took care of them and bought them everything they needed or wanted. Even though I am locked up, I still am able to provide for all three of my children. That is something that the system and no one else can ever take from me.

EPILOGUE TO MOUTHPIECE

Many of you may wonder a few things about me. You might ask yourself if I have such an attitude, and feel the way I do towards women, why then is it so damn easy for me to get them and to get them to do what I say? Why is it that they come running when I call them?

I am going to reveal to you a secret. The key is to get into their heads. You have to captivate their minds. Now I know some guys think that they have this mastered, and they might on some level, but it goes much deeper.

See, you have to captivate a woman on three levels: you have to seize her mentally, elevate her emotionally, and satisfy her physically.

Mentally, you seize her by the things you say, how you say them, and what images the words you speak create in her mind. They will either draw her to you or push her away from you. A woman's mind is like a rare jewel, you need to polish it so that its brilliance can truly shine.

Emotionally, you have to elevate her. You have to make her feel the things you say. You have to wrap her up in your mouthpiece. She has to feel like everything you say is to be valued like gold.

You need to connect with the wide range of emotions that she will express. You have to convince her that you are there to comfort her. See, one minute she can act blissful as if she is on cloud nine. She will even convince you that she is in heaven. Then, the next minute, she can act resentful. She can make you feel like the wrath of God is coming down upon you. Her emotions are a minefield that you have to know how to navigate through. You make one false move and you will blow everything up.

This is the most delicate side of the entire process. Everybody has heard the saying that there is nothing like a woman scorned. If she feels that you are trying to play her, she will burn you in more ways than you could ever think possible.

Now physically, there really is no one way to explain this instruction. Still, I know that most men have this twisted. They really don't have a clue as to how to conquer a woman and dominate her to the point where she is like putty in your hands. Yes, everybody knows how to fuck, but the key is to connect with the mental and emotional first. Once you do this, the physical will be over the top. You have to be extraordinary and know how to make her lose her mind. I make a woman hunger for me. I create a longing inside of them. I then help them to realize that the only person who can fill that void is me. And if, for any reason, she feels she does not have a void, I convince her that she does.

See, people have to realize that pimping is basically all about the mouthpiece. It is what you say and how you say it. It is detailing and giving a picture of life, in your own words. It is selling that picture and letting them know that the only way they can obtain that picture is through you.

I create a bridge and let a woman know that once she crosses that bridge, it is no longer about just her. It is now about her seeing us as a team. And, not just any team, but a winning team.

This pimping thing is like running a store. And I am an entrepreneur. When you run a store, you put out your products. The products that sell the best are the ones that the customers want the most.

There is no better product in the world than pussy. Pussy is what makes the world go around. If you have a top-notch hoe, then the customer is going to be willing to pay top notch money. If she is a bottom feeder, then the price is not going to be as much.

Let me ask, how many wars in this world be they big or small, do you think was started in some form or fashion, over a piece of pussy? Men have been killing each other since the dawn of time, over some pussy. They have been bending over backward just for a piece of pussy.

Pussy is like buying a pair of shoes. To get the brand new Jordans or Steph Curry's on the market, you are going to pay top dollar for them. Hell, Nike has this concept down. But, if the shoes are not new, then nobody is going to pay you top dollar for them.

If a hoe is dirty and the pussy stank, then she is not going to bring you any money. This shit is just common sense. Yet, at the same time, a true player in this game is not going to turn down the dollar. He is not going to say no to the dollars that a bottom-feeding hoe is going to drag in.

Unlike most dudes, I do not stick my dick in none of these hoes. It ain't about that. For me, it is always about the dollar. And, I cannot emphasize the following point enough, it is all about the mouthpiece. Yeah, I know that they want me, and I use this to my advantage, but I never lose sight of the fact that it is about the money. I keep feeding them a dream. I let a hoe know that even getting to have a glimpse of this dick, let alone getting to have it, is a privilege.

✖ ✖ ✖

Now with regards to the mothers of my children, my relationship with them was different. We were on a different level than I was on with a hoe that I was pimping. With each one of my baby mothers, there was something to me that was new and attractive. Even with that being said, however, when things went bad between us, they went all the way bad. Yes, we had our ups and downs, just like any couple does. My BM's and I were connected to each other with a level of understanding that what I did, my pimping, was what I did, and completely separate from our own romances, or so I thought.

My first BM, I will not mention any of their names, understood this perfectly at the beginning of our relationship. She knew what I did and was down with it. Hell, there were times when she would even help me pick up women and recruit them into the fold. She would be my point woman and even would spit game to the women for me.

There were times when I would be halfway across the city and she would call me and tell me that she had a bitch waiting for me. When I say that she was down with me, I mean that on every level. Hell, she would even lace them up on how to fuck a man right so to get him hooked.

It is crazy because one minute she was in it with me full force, then the next minute she flipped out on me. That is why I said that a woman's emotions are like a minefield.

She really started tripping out on me. All at once, she decided that she was no longer down with what I did. She acted like what I did was an excuse for me to be fucking with someone else. And, she thought that if that happened, she would end up losing me. She thought that I would no longer have an interest in her.

In no way did she ever stop to think that, or realize that, my dick is not attached to any type of feelings. Hell, the only thing besides my body that it is attached to is money.

See, it is a fact that very few women can actually have sex, and have it on a regular basis, without having their feelings get involved. Most women, some on their first time, get attached and they equate those feelings with love. They automatically assume that the man is experiencing these same feelings. Most of the time, they are dead wrong!

The only women I know who can have sex with a man and actually keep their feelings separated from the act is a hoe. They have mastered the art of simply fucking. Most people can find something negative to say about a hoe, but can't nobody accuse them of being over emotional women that have to cling to a man.

My BM never wanted to share me. And, she wasn't. She was just having a hard time seeing things that way. Because of this, we eventually grew apart.

I can say that she gave me a most precious gift. She gave me my first child. For all of her shortcomings, she is an excellent mother.

✖ ✖ ✖

My second BM was a dream woman. I loved everything about her. It may sound funny, but I also loved everything that she wasn't. By that, I mean, she was not always running around in the streets. She was not a club rat or a party girl that had to be out all day and night. Also, she was the kind of woman who listened to her man. That is a rare thing to find these days. Most women act as if they not only know all of the answers, but that they know the questions even before they are asked. They are stubborn, thick-headed, and act as if they have the world all figured out.

My second BM was faithful to me and had a rare quality of being loyal. There was no doubt that she was committed to me. For me, however, she had one gigantic flaw, she just was not nasty enough for me.

See, there are things that I was accustomed too that she was not doing. She was not showing me that freaky side that I needed. She was not making or keeping our sex life exciting.

Now I am sure that in time, I could have shown her how to fulfill my every need, and she probably would have been interested in learning, but I was not into teaching. I was a very impatient man.

Plus, I was too caught up in the streets and chasing money. I could not put in the time that was needed to cultivate her to my desired taste. I was not about to slow down and miss out on getting my money.

The crazy thing about us is, neither of us actually broke things off. We simply drifted apart. Looking back on it, I can pinpoint the start of our decline to the time her house got shot up one night while we were asleep.

About that night I don't remember much except going to sleep with her beside me. The next thing I know, she was shaking me awake and saying that the house was being attacked. My first thoughts were that she was joking and trying to see if she could scare me; then, I heard the shots for myself. I bolted out of the bed. I could smell in the air the scent of guns having been fired. I do not know exactly how long they shot up the house but it seemed as if it went on for forever. I instantly knew that it was one of my enemies retaliating and trying to catch me slipping.

Once it was over, I was out in the streets. I was looking for some get-back. It was crazy because I could not find anyone. Usually, you would see fools all over the place just hanging out and shooting the shit, but on that night, the streets were like a ghost town. I was already pissed off for being shot at, and not being able to strike back only increased my anger.

My BM called her dad and he came to pick her up. He and I never really got along, and probably never will. He always thought that I was not good enough for his daughter. I did not give a damn about him or his opinions.

It was not long after that incident that she and I sort of drifted apart. I was so caught up in the streets that I did not spend much time with her or the baby. She was fed up and was missing her family. She ended up moving further away and took the baby with her. I just shrugged it off and got myself deeper and deeper into the streets. It became so normal to me that the streets are where I stayed. I kept doing what I do best and I got me another bitch.

There is no doubt in my mind that had things gone a different way between the two of us, she would be here with me right now. She was the type of woman that would ride for me through thick and thin.

I know that she actually hates me right now because I ended up having another baby by someone else. Yet, at the same time, who I am, and the way I carry myself, along with this pimping game I got down to a science, has a hold on her heart that she will never be able to shake, no matter how hard she tries.

She knows that she will never be able to find another man who can even come close to comparing to who I am. I function on a level that is beyond her understanding. I do not yield to the things that most men do.

✖ ✖ ✖

Men are emotional creatures as well. We go through changes just like women do. We have our ups and downs, our good and our bad days. The thing is, a lot of men are just as good as hell at hiding it. I am an expert.

I am a master at both manipulating emotions and getting a woman to see things my way. I can smile in a person's face, pat him on the back and make him think that everything between us is all good while, at the same time, the anger in my heart is growing with each passing second. Homie would never have a clue as to the firestorm brewing inside of me.

I know for a fact that the moment a man just let's go and begins to get all emotional, one of three things happen: first, he gets eaten alive by other men. He becomes a laughing stock. In their eyes, he is a sucka. He is considered a chump. He is labeled as a bitch or a pussy. Everybody starts to treat him like he is as soft as cotton.

Now in response to that, those men usually become even more emotional as they try to defend themselves. They start to lash out and expose themselves to even more ridicule. That is when the cycle repeats itself.

Second, they are looked upon as a pushover. Most women will eat a weak ass man alive. They will run all over him. It will not take long before the roles in the relationship are switched and she will be wearing the pants. She will be calling the shots and controlling the relationship.

And, not only that, she will start talking all crazy to him and lose all form of respect for him. She will start raising her voice and getting all loud and disrespectful toward him. Hell, she might even start putting her hands on him if she deems him weak enough to take it. I know a whole lot of women who are capable of kicking a man's ass if he gives them a chance.

Third, he loses all manner of respect for himself. As far as I am concerned, this is the worst of the three. If, as a man, you have no respect for yourself, then you cannot expect for other people, no matter who they are, to respect you.

Now I know that because I was not willing to become all emotionally caught up with my second BM, she felt as if maybe I did not care about her as much as I did, but that is not true. It is funny because although we speak, we don't actually talk. Now what I mean by that is, whenever I call her, we will speak to each other, but all of our words are shallow and have no deep meaning to them. If I was to ask her how her day has been, we both know that I would not be asking because I cared. I would only be asking just to have something to say. She knows that I really do not give a damn. And, it is vice versa. She does not ask me anything serious because we both know that she could care less. The only serious topic of discussion between the two of us is my daughter. My BM tries to act as if she does not care that I am so invested in my child, but I know that she does.

Hell, there are thousands of men who are not locked up and can provide everything in the world to their children. They can spend quality time and give them all the nurturing in the world that the child needs growing up. Yet, these sorry ass nigga's do not even take advantage of the chances they are given.

I would give anything in the world to be in their shoes. Fuck the bitches, it is all about the kids. They need the guidance. A hoe is going to be a hoe and that is just the way it is.

With that being said, I will say this, I do not in any way, regret my third child, but I definitely regret my third child's BM. She put me through a roller-coaster ride. She was the absolute definition of a computer love.

I met her ass on Instagram. I saw a photo of her and was like, "Damn, I got to have her." She was fine as hell. When I say I had to have her, I mean that I really did have to have her.

She was young, smart, gorgeous, sassy, quick-witted, and most importantly, she was eager to learn. She stayed trying to get in the game. She was always trying to stick by my side when I was out in the streets. She was like a sponge soaking up this pimping game, but by catching this case, I ended up leaving her out there in the world to the wolves. And, like anybody that lay down with dogs, she picked up her own fleas. By that, I mean that she ended up acting like all of those no-good ass hoes out there.

Now, she's a hoe. She won't work. She refuses to get a job. And, whenever life circumstances and being broke force her to get one, she cannot keep it. All she wants to do is sit around on her ass all day, or be out running in the streets. She acts as if she does not have a care in the world.

The worst thing about all of this is, when it comes down to taking care of my child, she acts as if she does not have any form of parental instincts. She is not doing any of the things that a mother is supposed to do to teach a girl how to be a lady. But, I guess I cannot really expect for her to because she does not have a clue as to how a lady is supposed to act. She has never been one.

I know that if it was not for my daughter's grandmother, my daughter would be lost. She would be a wild child. Her grandmother does all of the things for her, that her mother should be doing. Her grandmother is filling in the gaps.

Even though I despise how my BM treats our daughter, the two of us remain cordial. We communicate, and when we do, I try to keep the arguing down to a minimum. I do not hate her, after all, I just do not like her.

I know that in her heart, she would want to get back with me if she had the chance, but I could never see that happening again. I do not go backward when it comes to relationships. Plus, knowing now that she is a hoe, it could never be the same.

As I think about things, I realize that with each one of my BM's, as with most women that I have had in my life, I eventually moved on from them because they started to lie and become manipulative. They all understood my lifestyle and what I was about, but as time went on, each of them became jealous, in their own way. They started wanting more and more of my time. They tried to smother me and force me to choose between them and the other women in my life, or choose between them and pimping. For sure, the pimping won out always.

But, by me knowing how they were thinking, I wound up manipulating them and playing them against each other. For example, one of them might have something that I wanted, so during that time, I would focus my attention on her. I would give her quality time and make her feel as if she was the only one. I would give her a false sense of hope. I caused her to think that she had won me over the others.

Knowing that they were mostly sexually motivated, I would also use this to my advantage. I knew that they wanted me, but that the more I held out, the hungrier they would be and the more eager they would become to satisfy my every need. It was all a matter of playing with their minds.

I also knew that none of them got along with the others so I would stir up the jealousy pot and have them ready to tear at each other's throats in order to have me for themselves. If one of them saw a photo of me on the other's Facebook page, or on Instagram or something like that, they would go into a rage. They would try to outdo the other to win my satisfaction.

While I was out on the streets, I had them in line, but now that I am locked away, for the time being, they do whatever in the hell they want to do. They are at each other's throats on social media. They are talking shit about me and the way that I treated them, yet at the same time, they are each claiming to be the one for me and to be with me.

Since I have been locked up, I have asked them to try and get along if for no other reason than for the sake of my kids. I want my children to know their siblings. Everybody in the world knows the damn saying about a woman being scorned. She will do whatever she has to do to enact revenge in some sort of way. And, that means that she will even use your kids against you if she has too. There is no limit to the ammunition that women will use.

Now there is no doubt that most of the stuff that they are doing they are only getting away with it because I am locked up. If I were out, I would make sure that my kids were around each other every day. They would be spending quality time together.

Each of my BM's told me that they felt betrayed by me because of how I ended up getting my next BM pregnant. I cannot understand it because all of them hoes act like they were not out in the streets doing their own thing. In the end, I know that it does not even matter because they are all out there screwing around with someone else.

✖ ✖ ✖

As I have said before, my kids are my world. My oldest, my son, Lil. O, is my ride or die. When I was out on the streets and doing my thing, I kept him with me as much as possible. He was on the track with me when I was running them hoes. He was riding with me when I was doing my thug thing. And, he was always learning how to be just like his daddy.

I remember the feelings that came over me when he was born. I was in the delivery room and cut the umbilical cord on him. I felt like for the first time in my life, everything was right in the world. When I saw his little face, my heart burst with pride. He looked exactly like me. I felt like no matter what, I had a legacy in him. I had a purpose.

Now I could not verbally express these feelings because, at the time, I did not know how too. Giving voice to the things I was experiencing was not a common occurrence. Hell, nobody in my family ever visibly showed emotions like that. I was never exposed to that sort of thing. And, I know that if I had been, I would have looked upon that person and labeled them as being a soft ass punk.

The crazy thing is, just as soon as those good and happy feeling began to settle into my mind, they were overshadowed by feelings of worry and doubt. I knew that the main thing for me was to now be able to provide for my son. I had to figure out how I could get some money and I had to do it quickly. I was broke and had a new mouth to feed.

I was coming from the bottom of the bottom and had absolutely nothing. I do not think that we even had a can of soup to eat at the time. We had no outside support. I was not working and she had no government assistance. Hell, we were the worst of the worst.

At this point in my life, I was at a real crossroads. I was caught up between thugging and pimping. I was on the fence and had one foot planted on each side.

Now, most people cannot understand this and do not know the difference between the two. Thugging means that I was caught up in the streets. I was actively engaged in the gang life. It was by far, more enticing to me. I was hanging out with my homies, getting high, and smoking weed on a daily basis. I was doing a lot more dirt. I was going out on missions. Hell, I even saw and was there when a lot of my homies got killed.

As crazy as this may sound, there is a lot more appeal to being in this lifestyle than most people would think. That is why there are so many young, black men who are out there grinding in the streets getting their paper and making a name for themselves in their hoods. This lifestyle has an attraction like none other. And, though many of these square' ass dudes in this world will not admit it, they too are enticed by this lifestyle. The world is seduced by the thug lifestyle. If it was not, then why are there so many people emulating the thug lifestyle? Why are there so many movies being made about it? Why are so many songs being written and sung about it? And, why are so many videos being produced depicting the lifestyle?

Women love bad boys. They are turned on by gangstas. They throw themselves at the thugs of the world.

Not only that, but there are far too many men to count that pattern themselves after gangstas. At the same time, there are so many suckas in this world who actively hate on thugs. They will go out of their way to try and throw salt on the game. They are the true definition of the term HATERS.

So, as a thug and having a newborn baby, I had to head out and hit the streets and make me and mines some money like never before. I did whatever I needed to do. I had to provide my son with formula to eat, pampers to put on his ass, and clothes, shoes, and a roof over his head. By doing so, my boy grew up seeing the game first hand. He had a respect for it and he imitated his dad.

I recall a time when I took him to Walmart with me. On that day, I found out how much like his dad he really was. We were walking down one of the aisles and I saw this fine ass woman in front of us. I mean she had an ass big enough to eat off of. She was sexy as hell. Just as we were walking past her, my son put his hand up her skirt and touched her on the butt. She instantly turned around and looked at me, assuming that I had done it. I explained to her that it was my son who had touched her, and she laughed. My son put on this cute, innocent looking face and then smiled. The lady was like putty in his hands. She bent down and gave him a hug and a kiss on the cheek.

I told him, "Boy if you keep this shit up, you are going to have me sent to jail." I was so proud of him. I knew that he had the pimping blood flowing through his veins. He was on track to be a real pimp. I do not think that I could have steered him in any other direction even if I wanted too. From that day forward, I kept him exposed to the game.

Now with my second child, my first daughter, the very first thought that crossed my mind when she was born was that I was going to need a bigger gun than the one that I had. I knew that I was going to have to go all out in protecting her. She was the most beautiful child I had ever seen. I knew that she was coming into an evil world. A world that would have no mercy on her or show any type of weakness. I knew that there were those in this world who would not hesitate to steal the innocence from her life. I was not having it.

Not only did I know that I needed a bigger gun, but I also knew that it was up to me to teach her about the true ways of the world. While other people were allowing their kids to live in a fantasy, I knew I had to give her the real so that she would not fall for the bullshit that was sure to come.

Also, I knew that she needed someone in her life that could teach her how to be a little lady. Her mother was perfect for that. She would definitely steer my daughter in the right direction. My only worry in that was that I did not want my daughter to become dependent on a man for any reason.

Now lastly, with regards to my third child, my second daughter, I was not on the streets when she was born. In turn, that made me feel like I needed not only a bigger gun, but two bigger guns.

I regret that I missed out on her birth. I know that I need my freedom to be able to protect her. I am hurting every day that I am not there to fulfill my duties as a father. I cannot say much about her because I am behind these bars and the loss I feel by not being in her life is a heavyweight that I carry each and every day. I want more than anything to get out there and show all of my children that their father is down for them.

38 YEARS LATER: BOOK FIVE OF THE MY CRIME SERIES PREVIEW

FORWARD TO 38 YEARS LATER

Brian Shipp is a risk taker. He skis black diamond slopes, throttles fast moving motorcycles, and cherishes the thrill of an occasional misdeed. He is a young man with a twinkle in his eye and a propensity for getting caught. Through hard work and charm, he races his way to the top, only, time after time, to find himself crashing down due to ill-conceived schemes.

"38 Years Later" is a post-modern tale of a youth from a broken background making sense of the world by giving his all to every endeavor, be it unlawful or good-natured. It is the tale of a life in progress, to this day.

Brian is the youngest child of three in a tradition-minded middle-class family that disintegrates during the days of the 1960's cultural shift. Similar to the times, Brian lives a life split between quicker, easier, yet riskier means of moving forward, namely illicit activities, and the steady character and work ethic he inherited from his father.

Brian is not all strength nor immune to loss. The loss of a unified family and later, in his teenage years, a loss of a strong sense of personal identity form trying times for a gifted young man pulled by opposing internal dialogs on how to establish himself in the world.

"38 Years Later" covers two periods in Brian's life, before prison and life in prison. The before prison story takes the reader through Brian's upbringing and early life choices while living in the San Francisco Bay Area. The before prison story also covers in detail the extraordinary play-by-play of Brian's 1980 commitment offense, an offense for which he remains in prison today.

The life in prison story reveals how time does not stop when men face the world in shackles. Follow Brian as he states his nuptial agreement in the confines of prison. Laugh with Brian as his firstborn "springs a leak," while having his diaper changed in the prison visiting room. Work with Brian as he builds a business from prison that makes it possible for his family to purchase their California home. Finally, stand with Brian as it all crashes down.

Brian's story is a tale of redemption and a tale that exemplifies the enduring character of human hope.

The East Oakland Times, LLC welcomes you to purchase the book today. "38 Years Later" can be found on Amazon, Audible, and at www.crimebios.com

✖ ✖ ✖

38 Years Later

In 1993, I had my life in order. I went to my scheduled progress hearing. The Parole Board found me suitable to be released into society. Everyone was so excited, including me. During this period the governor can revoke your parole grant basically for whatever reason he deems. This was a very scary period due to no lifer, at that time, ever clearing the governor's signature. We were called "political prisoners." As it happened, the governor denied my parole.

I lost hope as a result. I felt powerless. I truly felt that I would never see society or home. I began using drugs as a comfort and, eventually, spiraled into misery and started heavy drug use. I called my family and friends and told them I was never coming home. I told both not to write to me anymore, and, by then, I was no longer contacting them. I slowly became a drug addict.

During this period life was overwhelming. Crack and meth use was a daily thing for me. To make matters worse, I was just getting out of Administrative Segregation, the hole, after four months. I had been charged with "Conspiracy to Commit Bodily Injury to a Correctional Officer." That was a serious offense. Apparently, a black prison gang called 415 had plans to commit the act. I truly had nothing to do with the conspiracy. Nor did I have a residue of knowledge about the conspiracy yet I had to endure the entire disciplinary process. Prison staff were to investigate the likelihood of the conspiracy. Meanwhile, I was in a cell 23 hours a day. Please know that in prison, you're guilty until proven innocent. Eventually, the pain ended. I was cleared of the rules violation and, without an apology, released back to the mainline.

Now everything I had accomplished was gone. By being in the hole I lost my prison job and my hobby shop woodwork enterprise. I needed a new income source. Prison offers opportunities for revenue, either legal or illegal. I chose the legal realm. I knew a guy that had a few TVs stocked up. I propositioned him to buy the TVs at a discounted price. I slowly began to buy 13-inch color TVs and rent them out to other inmates. All the enterprise required was for me to keep an inventory of how many TVs were rented out, to whom the TVs were rented out, and the balance owed to me by each renter. I had a monthly rental fee of two cans of Bugler tobacco. Cans of tobacco sold for $5 at this time. At my peak, I owned and rented out 22 13-inch TVs. I acquired that many TVs in one years time.

The TV repairman had 16-inch color TVs that he wanted me to rent out for him. He didn't like dealing with inmates because of the games they played. I agreed to do so. I also needed his help to maintain my own TVs. Thus, with the additional 16-inch TVs, I was renting approximately 38 TVs on a monthly basis.

The income was great. I was profiting on average 60 cans of Bugler at $5 a can so basically a $300 monthly cycle. I still needed to expand. I created a T.V. guide business and had 145 customers. They each paid a pouch of Bugler a month, which cost $1.45. The T.V. guide business brought in revenue of $210 a month. From both endeavors, I was making $510 a month.

The TV enterprise was how I supported myself and my ever growing crack and meth habit. I understood I should have been sending the money home, but drugs had me. I couldn't wait to get back to my cell to get high. There were small clusters of inmates lined up outside my cell waiting on me. They knew my money was good. I would easily spend a couple hundred a week getting high.

Inmates are either bussed here or arrive in a van, as San Quentin is a Northern California reception center. San Quentin also serves to house general population inmates and holds the men on California's Death Row.

The inmates that were lined up outside my cell generally had some connection to the reception inmates. The reception inmates came directly from the county jails or other prisons. Drugs were clandestinely transported by reception inmates to San Quentin. New batches of prisoners came through Monday through Friday yet drug contraband arriving with them was never guaranteed. There were days when nothing came in. We called them "dry days." Dry days happened mostly on weekends when no new arrivals pulled up.

Dealing with my addiction was rough during those dry periods. The quality of the crack and meth also varied. Some of the stuff was really good; other times you got crap. I had various connections to ensure that I got the best. Of course, I had inmates who had their old ladies bring drugs in through the visiting room also. I did everything under the sun to get high.

EAST OAKLAND TIMES, LLC

The East Oakland Times, LLC (EOT) is a multi-media publication based in the San Francisco Bay Area. Founded by chief editor, Tio MacDonald, EOT has at its core three principles: the principle of the dignity of life, the principle of liberty, and the principle of tolerance. EOT supports the flourishing of civilization through the peace found by honoring these three stated principles.

Current Projects Include:

- Publishing of the My Crime Series
- The Publication of Original Inmate Art and Books
- Podcasts from California's Condemned Row
- Quarterly Print Publication for Free Distribution on the Streets of East Oakland
- Website Dedicated to Inmate Reporting on Current Events

Please remember by leaving a review you encourage others to buy the books in the My Crime series and thereby YOU support EOT's mission.

For exciting My Crime series bonus materials, such as original documents used for the composition of the book, go to www.crimebios.com

Support the EOT by purchasing EOT produced e-books, print

books, and audiobooks!

Stay positive & productive!

Unity in purpose!

Tio MacDonald
East Oakland Times
Chief Editor

EAST OAKLAND